# Africa's Living Arts

# Africa's Living Arts

## BY ANTHONY D. MARSHALL

ILLUSTRATED WITH PHOTOGRAPHS

Franklin Watts, Inc.
575 Lexington Avenue
New York, N.Y. 10022

1970

77-1840

*To Tee*

Map by George Buctel

SBN 531-01838-5

Library of Congress Catalog Card Number: 72-100091
Copyright © 1970 by Franklin Watts, Inc.
Printed in the United States of America
1   2   3   4   5

# Contents

# Africa's Living Arts

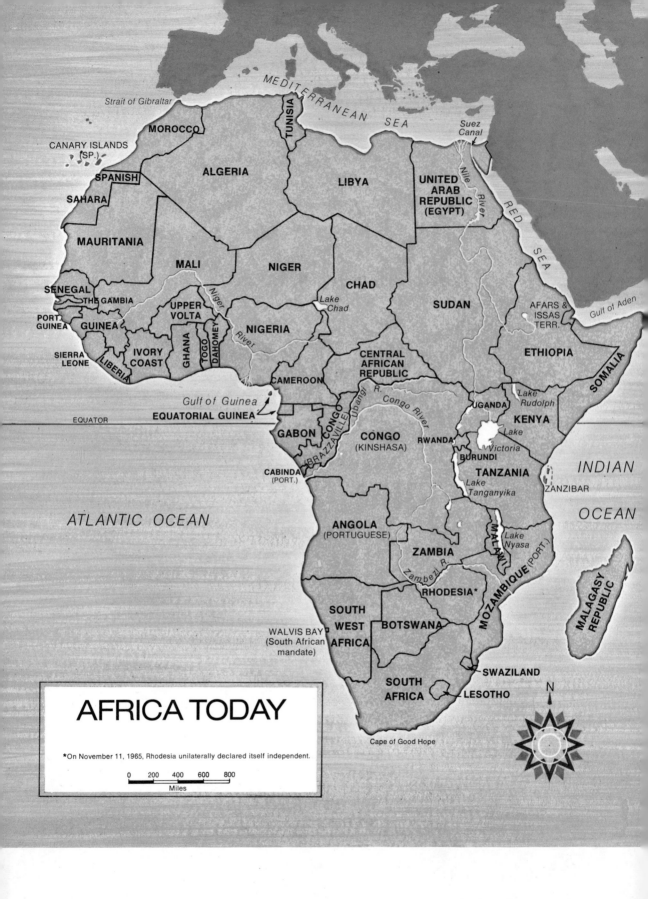

Strait of Gibraltar

MEDITERRANEAN SEA

CANARY ISLANDS
(SP.)

MOROCCO

TUNISIA

Suez
Canal

SPANISH

ALGERIA

LIBYA

UNITED
ARAB
REPUBLIC
(EGYPT)

SAHARA

Nile River

RED SEA

MAURITANIA

MALI

NIGER

CHAD

SUDAN

SENEGAL

THE GAMBIA

Lake
Chad

AFARS &
ISSAS
TERR.

Gulf of Aden

PORT.
GUINEA

GUINEA

UPPER
VOLTA

Niger River

NIGERIA

SIERRA
LEONE

LIBERIA

IVORY
COAST

GHANA

TOGO

DAHOMEY

River

CAMEROON

CENTRAL
AFRICAN
REPUBLIC

ETHIOPIA

SOMALIA

Gulf of Guinea

EQUATORIAL GUINEA

Ubangi R.

Congo River

Lake
Rudolph

UGANDA

KENYA

GABON

CONGO
(BRAZZAVILLE)

CONGO
(KINSHASA)

RWANDA

Lake
Victoria

CABINDA
(PORT.)

BURUNDI

TANZANIA

INDIAN

ZANZIBAR

Lake
Tanganyika

OCEAN

ATLANTIC OCEAN

EQUATOR

ANGOLA
(PORTUGUESE)

ZAMBIA

MALAWI

Lake
Nyasa

MOZAMBIQUE (PORT.)

Zambezi R.

RHODESIA*

MALAGASY
REPUBLIC

SOUTH
WEST
AFRICA

BOTSWANA

WALVIS BAY
(South African
mandate)

SWAZILAND

SOUTH
AFRICA

LESOTHO

Cape of Good Hope

N

# AFRICA TODAY

*On November 11, 1965, Rhodesia unilaterally declared itself independent.

0    200    400    600    800

Miles

# Introduction

Art in Africa has always been mainly functional. It thus exists as a vital part of everyday life, inseparable from the performance of daily tasks and the fulfillment of man's needs. It has been related to clothing, housing and household objects, religious and ceremonial practices, economic needs, transportation, wars and the hunt, and entertainment. Art objects always have served a purpose in African society. The fact that they were appealing to look at was of secondary importance. These objects were not made solely for art's sake, although today collectors of African art see in these objects the beauty of the culture and the historical significance that they represent. Most recently art has come to function commercially; that is, objects are being made in Africa purely for sale, mostly abroad. Each of these functions will be discussed in this book, after a look at old Africa. It is important to keep in mind that the functional art of Africa still lives. Articles attributed to a certain tribe are still being made by members of that same tribe.

Most books published today on African art concentrate on the "new art" or the "old art" or a particular type of art (there are many books on African sculpture or wood carving), or are restricted geographically to a particular area of Africa. This book takes a different, broad, comparative look at art in the whole of "black" Africa, the land that lies south of the Sahara Desert and north of the Republic of South Africa.

The art that is shipped to places outside of Africa, especially to the United States, is often manufactured for export and is designed for foreign tastes and use. Of the objects that are referred to as "old," most have been in existence for only thirty years or so. Many of the real antiquities of Africa have already been taken from the continent by colonialists or early visitors to Africa and are now in museums in Berlin, Dresden, Budapest, London, Paris, Vienna, Munich, or Liverpool. In some cases, as in Nigeria, where much of the best art had been removed by non-Africans before 1943, the government now has imposed heavy restrictions, including fines, on the export of antiquities. The Nigerians want to keep their art in their own country, where it can be displayed in their own fine museums, such as those in Lagos, Ife, and Jos.

The flood of African art items currently reaching the West causes many people outside the continent to think of art in Africa as new. This is not so. In the first chapter you will see just how old art in Africa really is. You will also learn something of events taking place in other parts of the world while African culture was developing. In reading the first chapter, it is not important to remember all the many facts and dates; instead, you should get a picture in your own mind of how old African culture actually is.

Do not forget that until fairly recently there were no airplanes, telephones, television sets, or satellites. The world has

An ancient Benin ceremonial bell (left) and a modern Benin brass figure of an *oba,* or king, holding his sword of authority.

shrunk greatly within the last generation. Just think of the speed with which a message or news can now get from one point to another. But, thousands and even hundreds of years ago, people were isolated from the rest of the world. It took a long time for new ideas to spread from one place to another. Historians are still learning how and when people traveled between different parts of the world, taking with them part of their culture. When they settled in new places, they would form new cultures, blending the culture they brought with them with the one they found in their new homeland. The Negroes, ancestors of the majority of black Africans today, came to the continent from Asia about 6000 or 5000 B.C. Bushmen, who were already in Africa, were pushed farther south. During the first millennium B.C., the Sabaeans arrived in the east. Trade started between East Africa and Asia sometime around the first or second century A.D., and the East Africans adopted the outrigger canoe of Indonesia. From the seventh century A.D. onward, the Arabs in their conquest of North Africa planted much of their culture, particularly religion, deep in the heart of Africa. The Europeans — Portuguese merchants, British traders, and French colonists in the early days, and later the Germans and Spaniards — brought new ideas with them to Africa. Later, in the first decade of this century, European artists, such as Picasso, "discovered" art in Africa and began to interpret in their own work what they saw. All of these points will be discussed in the following pages.

CHAPTER ONE

# Art in Ancient Africa

There are two questions that must be asked when we start our study of art in Africa. First, what *is* art? Second, what was happening in parts of the world other than Africa during the same period of history? The answers to these two questions give us perspective; we get a broader understanding not only of art and its development in Africa but of how Africa's historical development fits into world history. In studying art one studies the moods and activities of the people in history. Art reflects history; it is a visual account of history. Art is an expression of the culture of a society, a people. In studying African art, it is also important to know geography. You can then better understand what happened where and when. Without this, you learn isolated facts; they become important only when you put them together.

The first fact you should consider has to do with man himself. According to the latest scientific findings, man originated in Africa. In 1959, Dr. L. S. B. Leakey found the remains of oldest man, which he called *homo habilis,* in Olduvai Gorge in Tanzania. This man is 1,750,000 years old and is believed to be the world's first toolmaker.

| 13

Let us now leap hundreds of thousands of years to the fifth millennium B.C. At that time men were drawing pictures on stone in Africa. Cave paintings made by bushmen have been found in Angola and Southwest Africa. Others were found in the Tassili region of Algeria in 1909, and in northern Nigeria and nearby areas in Chad. These paintings date back to 5500 B.C. However, many of the rock paintings of early man in Africa have been hidden from modern man as the result of big shifts in the earth's surface, caused by water, wind, and surface movements coming from far below. This change in Africa's landforms has buried many art treasures, or accounts of the history of man, belowground at depths of from 15 to 60 feet, or more. Sometimes by luck ancient art is found; more often scientists, such as Dr. Leakey, spend years looking for the existence of ancient civilizations along escarpments, or cliffs, in such places as the Great Rift Valley, which stretches from the Dead Sea in Jordan (the Red Sea is part of it) to Malawi in southern Africa. Olduvai Gorge is in the Rift Valley.

Let us take another step forward in history to the year 2555 B.C. (this year was positively fixed by a carbon 14 test) and to the pottery found at Nsukka Farm site in the eastern part of Nigeria. At this same time in history the pyramids were being built in Egypt.

Another leap to 500 B.C., when the Nok culture, which existed from 900 B.C. to A.D. 200, was at its height in Nigeria. Evidence of this period can be found in pottery heads that served a religious function as a point of contact (an image) between the unseen world and the material one. At the same time, to the north, in Tondia, near Goundam in the country today

Dr. L. S. B. Leakey, who discovered "earliest man" of prehistory at Olduvai Gorge, Tanzania, in 1959 looks at the jawbone of a twenty-million-year-old bush baby (species of lemur) at an excavation site in Kenya.

called Niger, people were making rock engravings showing horsedrawn chariots. This tells us not only of their use of the wheel, but something of their lives, indicating that they were able to travel considerable distances. In Europe, Athens was at its cultural height in the fifth century B.C., and wooden statues were being replaced by those made of marble.

There is evidence (found by British archaeologist Graham Connah in 1965–66) that at Daima, in northeastern Nigeria, there was a thriving settlement from at least the fifth century B.C. to the tenth century A.D. Other evidence suggests that the settlement survived until the seventeenth or eighteenth century A.D. As reported in the October 14, 1967, issue of the *Illustrated London News,* "The occupants of the earlier settlements were a cattle-rearing people with polished stone axes, polished bone harpoons, and other bone tools. They made good pottery

Statue of a queen of Benin,
in Benin, Nigeria.

and, for some possibly religious purpose, miniature animal figures fired in clay; they buried their dead in a crouched or flexed position within the settlement. Sometime around the first century B.C., or first century A.D., the earliest iron arrived at the site and from then on, or soon after, bone harpoons and tools ceased to be made although the stone axes lingered on for some time."

Excellent examples of Nigerian bronzes, dating from A.D. 750 to 940, were found in what was probably a burial site. The bronzes had apparently been made locally; if they were not, they were imported from the east or north. Each of the items found seemed to have served a religious and ceremonial function in the society that made them.

We must digress a moment to study these bronze figures. First of all, consider the difference between bronze and brass. Bronze is composed of copper and tin, sometimes with a little zinc and lead. Brass, on the other hand, is composed of copper and zinc. Despite the difference, the terms "bronze" and "brass" are frequently used interchangeably. The ancient (fourteenth-century Ife and earlier; Benin, fifteenth–nineteenth century) bronze and brass figures of today were and are made in West Africa as far south as Angola by the "lost-wax process." This process consists of five steps: (1) The object is first modeled in beeswax with wax rods. (2) The model is coated with clay. (3) The model is dried and then heated so that the wax melts away and is lost. (4) Then the molten brass is poured in through the wax rods. (5) The metal hardens and the clay is removed and the rods are cut.

It is interesting to compare historical events; while bronzes

17

Brass figures representing a secret cult were made by the five-step lost-wax process and were used in religious ceremonies.

were being made in West Africa, Charles the Great (Charlemagne) ruled Europe (A.D. 771–814); and the Norsemen, under Eric the Red, discovered Greenland in 981. This was a period of inactivity for art in Europe.

From A.D. 1100 to 1400, Ife art in Nigeria was flourishing. Around A.D. 1100, Ghanaians were using iron and knew the art of making swords and lances to fight their enemies, who were armed only with wooden weapons; they also made nails, arrowheads, farming tools, and even scissors. These ancient Ghanaians painted stone and made pottery.

During the time of Ife art and the Ghanaians, the Crusades were were taking place in Europe (1096–1291); Genghis Khan (1162–1227) and Kublai Khan (1216–94) conquered Asia. Marco Polo, the great Venetian merchant, made his journey (1274) to Cathay (modern Peking). Oxford University began in 1167. Wax came into use for candles in the twelfth century in Europe, but they were considered a luxury.

Timbuktu, in the present-day country of Mali (formerly the French Sudan), began as a caravan and river trading center in the eleventh century, but flourished during the fourteenth century, while Europe was engaged in the Hundred Years' War, started with the English invasion of France in 1337. Timbuktu, on the banks of the Niger River, was a center for both Islam and commerce. It served as the focal point for the trade of goods and ideas flowing from the African Mediterranean coast (present-day Morocco, Algeria, and Tunisia) into the whole of West Africa.

The Benin Empire (Benin is now the capital of a province of the Western Region in Nigeria) lasted from about 1400 to 1600, and the mysterious city of Zimbabwe, in Rhodesia, with its granite-block walls, was a center of trade from 1250 to 1750. It was mysterious because apparently no one wrote about it; everything we know about this city has been learned from its ruins, which can be seen today.

In about 1600, King Shamba Bolongongo was the ninety-third ruler of the Bushongo tribe, which lived along the Sankuru River, a branch of the Congo River, in the center of what is now the Democratic Republic of the Congo (Kinshasa). (There are two "Congos" today: the Democratic Republic of

A Benin bronze head, about 400 years old. There are three periods of old Benin: (1) early (through the fifteenth century), made of thin castings in a naturalistic style; (2) middle (sixteenth through eighteenth centuries), made of heavy castings with a European influence; (3) late (nineteenth century), made with more elaborate designs.

the Congo, formerly the Belgian Congo, with its capital in Kinshasa, formerly called Léopoldville; and the Republic of Congo, formerly French Equatorial Africa, with Brazzaville as its capital.) King Bolongongo abolished his army and forbade knife-throwing in warfare. At the same time in history, in 1588 and again in 1624, England was at war with Spain; Italy had a war over the Mantuan succession (1627–31); and in England Henry VIII became head of the Church (1534) and beheaded Sir Thomas More (1535) and Queen Anne Boleyn (1536) and suppressed monasteries (1538). In America, Jamestown, Virginia, was founded in 1607. China was conquered by the Tatars, establishing the Tsin dynasty in 1616–44. Leonardo da Vinci (1452–1519) painted in Italy, where sculptor Benvenuto Cellini (1500–71) lived.

20

As a final note, it is important to realize that it is not only in Africa that functional objects are regarded as art. For example, displays in museums — and even entire museums — in the United States are devoted to recreating through functional art objects the life of colonial America or of American Indians. The same is true of other cultures throughout the world.

CHAPTER TWO

# Dress

The form of dress in Africa varies both with climate and with tribal customs, as well as with availability of materials. In spite of great differences in climate on the African continent, there are generally only two seasons, dry and wet. The rains in Cameroon are the heaviest in the world, with an average annual fall of 350 inches, while in comparison, New York City receives 42 inches. Most Africans dress according to climate: the warmer it is, the less they wear; however, there are contradictions. In some warm climates the people cover themselves for protection from the heat and sun, as do most Africans in Muslim areas, where the men wear long white robes and colorful turban headdresses.

Articles of clothing include those made of handwoven fabrics of cotton, silk, or wool; bark from the fig tree; skins, including cattle, goat, camel, and leopard as well as other fur-bearing animals; bamboo; shells or beads strung together; feathers, particularly as a headdress; and grass, sisal, or raffia.

Handwoven fabrics are made and worn predominantly in West Africa. Some of the best-known fabrics are the Akwete, Okene, and Asooke of Nigeria, Kente of Ghana, Ewe of Togo, and tie-and-dye, called Adire in Nigeria. The Ashanti people in Ghana make a patterned white cloth that is stamped with designs cut from a calabash, or gourd.

Akwete cloth is named after the town in eastern Nigeria where it is woven. Only women weave Akwete cloth, which is made of cotton in pieces (called "fathoms") the size of the loom, or about 48 inches by 72 inches. There are nearly two hundred different patterns or designs. Some have an abstract, geometric look about them, similar to Aztec Indian designs; others are woven with patterns that look like a sheaf of wheat, an hourglass, a chicken, an ostrich, or even designs of the Nigerian flag. The designs are named after people as well; one is named after the wife of the former President (Azikwe) of Nigeria. It takes three weeks to weave one fathom of Akwete cloth. Each fathom is a work of art. Women in southern Nigeria still use the Akwete cloth as clothing, wearing it wrapped around their waists as a skirt, usually with a European-style blouse as a top.

Asooke cloth is another interesting handwoven fabric. This is the Yoruba name (meaning "up-country") for a type of cloth woven on a loom found in many parts of Africa. In Sierra Leone it is called "mende cloth." The Ashanti of Ghana call it Adinkra. Cloths woven on a similar loom are found throughout West Africa, from Senegal to the Congo. The loom is also still used today in Somalia on the easternmost point of the continent. The cloth made on this type of loom measures only four to six inches wide, but can be as long as ten yards. It is very sturdy, being tightly woven, and frequently colorful. Sometimes "holes" are woven into the cloth as part of the design. The cloth

Asooke cloth, four to six inches in width and up to ten yards in length, is woven on a tight loom.

This headdress was made by sewing together several narrow strips of Asooke cloth.

is cut and the strips are sewn together into a larger piece that is then used in various forms as clothing.

Kente is an expensive, brightly colored silk cloth made in Ghana. The silk Lokoja and Okene cloths of northeastern Nigeria are made from *anaphe*, young moth caterpillars. Keta cloth is made by the Ewe tribe of Togo and resembles the Kente of Ghana.

The Adire cloth of Abeokuta, Western Nigeria, probably did not originate in Abeokuta. "Adire" is the name given this tie-and-dye process of the Egba tribe. Threads are woven — by hand — into a cloth that is then dyed. When it dries, the threads are taken out and a pattern is formed. There are many patterns; new ones are still being developed, but the process has remained the same over the years. The only change is in the dye used; vegetables dyes that were formerly used were not colorfast; the chemical dyes of today are, and they make the new fabric more wearable, lasting, and salable. Similar tie-and-dye cloth is made in Liberia and the Sudan and was found in the central part of West Africa as early as the sixteenth century.

Tie-and-dye "cloth" is also made out of raffia (palm leaves) as done by the Genya tribe of the east-central Congo and the Baule tribe of the Ivory Coast. In the island country of the Republic of Malagasy, silk *lambas*, or hanging shirts, and palm-fiber smocks are woven. Sometimes beads made from imported tin are worked into the "cloth."

In the ancient city of Kano, which dates back to A.D. 900, cotton cloth, soaked in large pottery vats that have been sunk into the ground, is usually dyed an indigo color. After it is dyed, the cloth is hung to dry, then beaten on a stone with a wooden

An indigo-colored cotton fabric is produced in the dyeing vats at Kano. When not in use, the vats are covered with inverted baskets.

stick to make it shine. The dyeing vats behind the city's mud-baked walls are a popular tourist attraction.

African fabric designs are often decorated with imaginative and even amusing embroidery. Frequently, embroidered cloth, such as that made in Dahomey, tells a story. In the hot and dry interior of West Africa one can find colorful designs that depict emirs (the kings of the north), camels, or unidentifiable figures embroidered into the cotton sheets, such as those made by the Hausa women of Kano. In the country of Niger one finds embroidered loincloths, while in the Federal Republic of Cameroon there are richly embroidered cloths with bead designs made in Bikom as well as the woven Kom cloth from Wum.

Africans are still weaving and wearing these handmade cloths. However, a change has come about. With the increased speed of communications, or transportation, and the worldwide increase in the cost of living, handmade articles are becoming more available but also more expensive. It still takes the same amount of time to handweave cloth as it always did, but modern machine-made cloths can be made quicker and cheaper. The handwoven cloths are becoming collectors' items. The result is that imported and locally manufactured cloth is replacing handwoven cloth. However, tradition is strong, and the machine-made cloths have patterns and colors that are African in origin and concept.

Another case in point is the *khanga* that is worn in East Africa, from Madagascar through Tanzania to Kenya, but is manufactured in the Netherlands, England, India, and Japan. The *khanga* has become a traditional dress in these African countries, and the selection of designs, color schemes, and combinations are African. The *khangas* even have sayings or proverbs printed on the cloth in the Swahili language.

There are a number of other sources of basic materials for clothing other than cloth. The Masai in Kenya and Tanzania are one tribe of Africans who have retained their original dress of leather or cloth sheets draped over their bodies. In Uganda and in Cameroon, the bark from a fig tree is beaten with wooden hammers and decorated and then worn as clothing. The Chagga of Tanzania wear sarongs made of hyrax (rock-rabbit) skins and goatskins dyed with red ocher. Leopard skins were, and still are — particularly in ceremonial activities — popular in East Africa, especially in Tanzania and Kenya, although they are also used in parts of the Congo and Rwanda and Burundi. Lion's-mane headdresses were worn by the Masai; originally a youth had to kill his own lion as an initiation into manhood. Near Lake Bangweolo in southeastern Congo a cloth made of marsh antelope is worn. The Ethiopians have used the skin of the Colubus monkey as decorative clothing. In most parts of Africa, dried and cured skins from cattle, goats, and camels are made into some form of clothing, including sandals. Bamboo is used in areas of the tropical rain forest for clothing, pieces being cut into small sections and strung together, then worn either hanging from the waist or even from the neck down beyond the waist. Shells, especially the cowrie shell, also strung, are used in much the same manner. Feathers, particularly ostrich, are used not only as a headdress but sometimes to decorate clothing. Grass (throughout Africa), sisal (in East Africa), and raffia (in West Africa) are made into

Figure of a Masai warrior in lion's mane headdress.

skirts worn by both men and women. At times these materials are wound around the ankles and arms.

One costume of West Africa, worn by the Yoruba tribe, deserves particular attention. The *agbada* is a three-piece suit: very baggy trousers, a loose shirt hanging outside the trousers, and on top of both an enormous cloth that envelops the man. Frequently geometric designs are embroidered on the cloth, which is made either of plain cotton fabric (usually white or blue, but sometimes yellow or tan) or of the narrow handwoven Asooke pieces that have been sewn together and then cut to size. An *agbada* costs from $40, for the very plainest, to $150 or more. These prices are high for a country such as Nigeria where the per capita income is $75 per year.

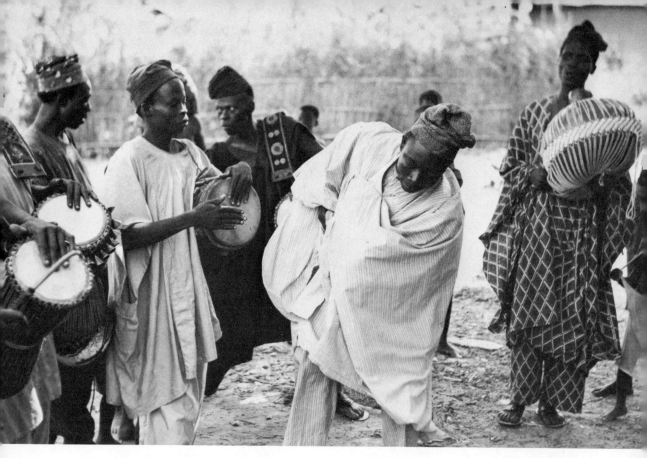

The *agbada,* a three-piece suit consisting of baggy trousers and a loose shirt covered by an enormous cloth, is the everyday dress for many West Africans.

The style of headdresses in Africa varies considerably. Basic materials for them are cloth, skins, feathers, grass, sisal, or raffia. What must first be pointed out regarding headdress is that sometimes the "dress" of the head is in the hairdo, or hairstyle, and not in the covering. Some people in the country of the Upper Volta wear straw hats with leather tops. Straw hats are worn by the Mandingos of Senegal, Guinea, and Mali, and plaited-straw caps are worn in Madagascar. In West Africa there are many styles of cloth hats. The Hausa wears a pillbox type of hat. The Yoruba tribe wears a flopover-style cap, usually made of Asooke.

Before leaving the subject of clothing, and in particular handwoven fabrics, it is important to note the weaving interest, skill, and development of the Navajo Indian in America. The Navajo, the largest American Indian tribe (numbering 80,000 today), used the wool of sheep they got from the Spanish and adopted the weaving techniques of the earlier Pueblo Indians. The blankets that they wove were used as clothing from 1700 until the early 1800's, when machine-made fabric became available. However, their art did not stop, and instead they loomed thicker cloth that was used in the making of rugs. There were about eighty recipes for the vegetable dyes used to color the wool. It takes a Navajo about 350 hours to weave a rug three by five feet, or just slightly longer than it takes a Nigerian to weave an Akwete fathom. With the Navajos, as with the Africans, the handweaving of fabric remains very much a living art.

This West African headdress, worn by a dancer, represents an ancestral *dodo* spirit, and is made of wood, skin, beads, and cord.

CHAPTER THREE

# Personal Ornaments

Personal ornaments in Africa were — and in many cases still are — a sign of wealth, authority, tribal association, social standing, or religious significance. Ornaments are worn about the neck, from or through the ear or lip (as plugs), and around the arms or hands. Very often pieces of jewelry, particularly of gold, are a sign of wealth. In some cases they are all that a person owns. At times a decoration has a purely functional purpose, such as the snuff containers that the Masai carry, hanging either from the ear, waist, or neck. Another example is the decorative container carried by a Muslim for his Koran, or holy book.

Materials used to make personal ornaments include ostrich eggshell, seeds, roots, cowries, beads, ivory, elephant and giraffe hair, iron, brass, and aluminum. Other materials used are seashells or small snail shells found attached to tree trunks during the rainy season, bone (usually of cattle, but also warthog), stone, brass (collars found in the Congo weigh up to 17 pounds or more), wood, silver, and gold. Many of the metals are made into necklaces that may often be either linked, carved, or engraved.

Kikuyu dancers in a small village outside Nairobi, the capital of Kenya.

*(Left)* A modern ebony carving of a jackrabbit, standing about fourteen inches high, is made for export. *(Above, right)* After thornwood is carefully carved, pieces are glued together to form figures. A raw, or uncarved, piece of thornwood can be seen on the far right. *(Below, right)* An East African Masai necklace.

The figures in this outdoor mural are performing everyday tasks.

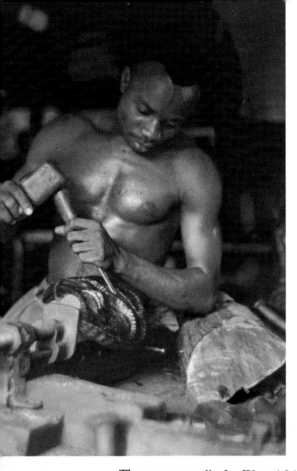

Putting the finishing touches on an ebony mask.

The average stall of a West African trader displays a variety of arts and crafts —
carvings, ivory, beads, leatherwork, and brass.

Dancers entertain a crowd gathered in Nigeria.

A Masai warrior in Tanzania.

Three different patterns of *Akwete* fabric, handwoven, to be made into clothing.

The northern Nigerian customarily dresses in white robes, but often wears flamboyant colors.

This Congolese oil-painting is the work of artist Nkoukou.

In many parts of Africa beads are used as personal ornaments. They are worn strung as a necklace or bracelet, woven into or part of cloth or raffia, or strung and tied into leather aprons hanging from a plaited hide waistband as done by the young Karamojong women in Uganda.

One of the most treasured types of beads of West Africa was the original Ghanaian blue *aggrey* bead. These "beads" were actually a river coral; that is, a part of a petrified tree at the bottom of a river. Nowadays the *aggrey* beads, still found

*Aggrey* beads make an attractive necklace.

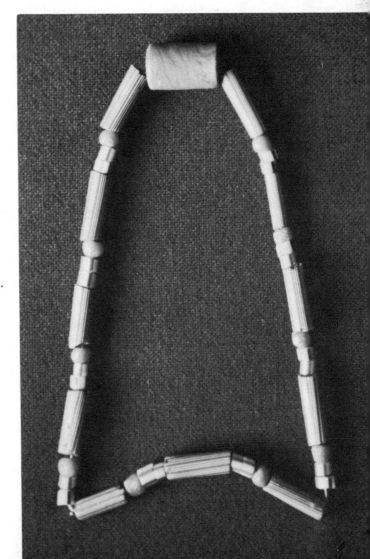

in parts of West Africa, are made of stone rather than coral and are cylindrically shaped and polished with a pattern that resembles a snakeskin.

An interesting type of bead necklace and bracelet found in Africa is made from an age-old glass process in the Nigerian city of Bida. Little is known of the original people who made these glass beads, although it is believed that they came from Egypt about two hundred years ago, passing through the present-day country of Niger. They were members of a guild called Larabawa, which is the Hausa tribe name for the Arabs. Glassmaking was a very secret art, and at first, guild members were not allowed to marry outsiders. Youths were not permitted to learn another trade. Until the end of the nineteenth century, all the glass produced was nearly black. Today the glass itself is not manufactured, and the raw material is obtained from bottles — mostly from beer and soft drinks — that are melted down and then used to make beads and other ornaments, and even glass figures of animals.

It takes a team of four men to make these glass beads. One man operates the bellows; of the other three who are around the hearth, one prepares the molten glass while the other two make the beads. As wood is added to the fire and the bellows are kept working, each beadmaker dips a three-foot rod into a bowl of mud so that the bead will not stick to the spit; then he scoops up a bit of molten glass, twisting the rod with his hand and shaping the glass over the flame. By striking the rod with a piece of metal, the glass bead is loosened and can be shaken off into a calabash bowl.

Anklets were usually made of metal and sometimes

A Fulani girl wearing Bida beads around her neck and Nigerian pennies on her headband of imported beads. *Photo courtesy of the Nigerian Ministry of Information*

weighed 13 pounds or more. Often coils of wire were worn, and bells were attached to them when the anklets were used for dancing. As the dancers moved their feet they also made a "musical" note, giving the basic beat or rhythm to the dance music. Or, as in the case of the Obas (kings) of southern Nigeria, anklets were worn as a sign of authority as well as for religious or ceremonial purposes. The same is basically true of armlets. Mention has already been made of the use of raffia for arm and ankle decoration.

Bracelets of many sorts have been used by Africans through the centuries. Ivory armlets were worn by the Chagga women of Tanzania. Today beaded bracelets, which have been worn by Africans for many years, have become increasingly popular with foreigners as well. Bracelets of interwoven hairs taken from the end of an elephant's tail are worn by African hunters who have killed an elephant themselves. Earrings are usually made from either brass, beads, wood, horn, tin, or gold.

It is important to remember that the ornaments a man or woman wears, as well as the way he or she is dressed, are determined by tradition, according to tribal customs. Dress and ornaments are a functional aspect of art as they were both a part and a result of tribal traditions. They reflected visually many of the deeply rooted ways and thoughts of African life. While change is coming rapidly to the cities of Africa, traditional beliefs and customs change less quickly. In the Africa of today we can still see the living arts of centuries past.

# CHAPTER FOUR

# Housing and Household Goods

The construction of traditional housing in Africa is determined primarily by two factors — the materials available and the need for protection. It is the latter that determines the style, or architecture, of a house.

Most common of the materials available are mud, grass, branches and sticks, palm leaves, and reeds. In areas of the tropical rain forest, which includes most of West Africa and some parts of Central Africa, there is an abundance of wood and vegetation. Therefore, the houses are built either with wooden walls and thatched grass and palm-leaf roofs, or with mud walls and thatched roofs. The thatched roofs have to be repaired frequently, but with care they provide as good a weather shelter as do the thatched huts along the Thames River in England. The wooden walls are made of sticks that are interwoven. Wood does not last long in most parts of Africa because of the termites and the climate; it seems as if the two are battling one another over which will destroy the wood first. For this reason it would be too impractical to use planks or poles of wood for walls or floors.

In parts of Africa, particularly in regions where there is

One example of thatched-roof huts, seen here in a small community in Uganda.

little or no vegetation, such as in some areas of northern Nigeria and in the countries of Mali, Upper Volta, and Niger, the houses are built entirely of mud. However, in parts of Chad, where grass is available, the roofs are thatched. The walls of the mud huts are most often painted with lime as a protection against the rain.

The major factor influencing the architecture of housing in Africa is defense — defense against the elements, or weather, and defense against alien humans and animals. The traditional architectural concept in building an African house is that it is

38

designed to provide shade, and — more important — to eliminate the glare of the sun. In most cases there is an overhanging roof, and sometimes a kind of portico that not only provides out-of-doors shelter during bad weather, but also provides the longed-for shade. Partly because of the need for protection from the outside, most traditional houses are part of a group within a compound, frequently with an inner courtyard or area for community use. In addition, there is often a wall enclosing the compound, sometimes of mud, at other times only of thornbushes. The wall is intended to keep domestic animals inside and intruders out.

Dried mud houses of Kano.

Let us examine one style of house made of mud by the Hausa tribe in Zaria in northern Nigeria, where the exteriors of the houses are attractively decorated with designs. To build a house out of mud is not an easy task; but through the centuries solid constructions have developed. The walls are of sun-dried, pear-shaped bricks, which are set one on top of the other, with their pointed ends facing upward. The flat roofs and first-story floors are done in the same manner, supported from beneath by flat mud arches, reinforced by split palm. In planning the construction of a home in Zaria (and this applies to nearly any home in Africa), four factors must be taken into consideration: privacy; a place to live, sleep, and eat; space for possessions, in particular, such animals as goats and sheep; and shelter from the sun and rain.

There is usually some decoration around the main entrance or door. Within the compound or house itself, there is rarely any wall decoration, as the decoration is made for others to see, not for the enjoyment of the owner. The designs on the walls of the Zaria houses are made completely by hand, without the use of any tools. Many of the older designs are thought to have originated in the Middle East. It is believed that Muslim converts in southern Africa journeyed to Mecca and brought the designs back to their homelands. Some designs resemble those found on leather Koran cases. One popular design is the old colonial Nigerian seal of interwoven circles: its origin is not known, although it is also believed to have come from the Middle East. The same design is used by carvers of the calabash.

Other forms of decoration are found within a compound. Take, for example, the palace of the Alake of Abeokuta, who

The old colonial Nigerian seal of interwoven circles, shown here as carved from a calabash fruit, is often used to decorate a house.

was once a powerful ruler in western Nigeria. The author has visited the present Alake, who still lives in the palace. Under a portico in his courtyard there are carved wooden figures that have both historical significance (they tell a story about the area's history, including the "coming" of the white man) and religious or ceremonial significance.

These painted wooden carvings of a chieftain stand in the courtyard of the palace of the Alake of Abeokuta, Nigeria.

Materials for building an *aghal,* the house of a Somali nomad, are "stored" for safekeeping either on the ground, surrounded by thornbush, or in a treetop.

In Somalia the people are nomadic, moving from one part of the country to another. Sometimes they carry sticks and branches with them on camels to use to construct their houses, called *aghals.* Often they store their construction materials in treetops, to prevent animals from carrying them away.

Many tribes of East Africa, such as the Masai, build their homes of dung and mud and grass, as round igloo-shaped huts with a tunneled entrance. There is no chimney, and when a fire is built the smoke fills the dwelling, escaping only through the tunnel entrance (and exit). Several of these *bomas* are grouped together into a compound, surrounded by a thornbush wall.

In other parts of East Africa are the Kikuyu, found in the highlands of Kenya, who build a tepee-style hut of wooden branches with a center pole; when the head of the family dies the pole is removed and the building is burned.

In Senegal, the Fulani build T-shaped huts of sticks and grass that are similar in appearance to the Masai *bomas*. In the southern and south-central parts of Africa are the *rondavel*, or

A Masai *boma,* a home found in East Africa, in Tanzania.

round one-room stucco huts with thatched roofs. In Dahomey, along the shore, people build houses on stilts, much like those built many years before Christ on the lakeshores of Switzerland, or still built today along the Amazon River in Brazil.

The European has had both a good and a bad influence on African houses and their architecture. Hardly worthy of classification as architecture, but certainly a result of European influence, are tin-roofed structures found throughout Africa, particularly in the poorer areas. The metal lasts far longer than mud, sticks, or straw, but the aesthetic appeal — the art of indigenous handmade manufacture — is gone.

Enter a house; take a look inside.

Arrangement of the interior varies, but the traditional African house has a dirt or mud or, more recently, cement floor. A grass, sisal, or raffia rug covers part of the floor and may be used to sit on. Camel's hair rugs are found in Chad and Niger. In Ethiopia, however, skins such as those of the Colobus monkey are made into a rug, several being placed together. Thick handwoven cotton rugs are also used. Again, it is important to remember that we are speaking of the traditional African house, which is still found almost everywhere in Africa — not only in rural areas, but in the poorer sections of cities, as well.

Every home has a cooking and sleeping area. Weather permitting, the cooking is done outside over an open fire. A few stones are put together, or perhaps a grate is used; a pot hangs over the fire or is placed directly on it. There is always a grinding stone for the *gari*, which is cassava made into flour, and

A simple Somali stove has a metal container as its base.

Grinding cassava flour, or *gari,* is still done the traditional way in many parts of Africa.

a wooden container usually about two feet high for the pounding of yams, which is done with long poles by the women. It is interesting to note that the Museum of Natural History in New York City has an exhibit showing the early American Indian tribe of Iroquois using their mortar and pestle, which very closely resemble the African yam containers, to pound corn. African pot covers are most often made of very tightly woven grass, usually decoratively colored, although metal, including enamelware, is also used nowadays. A calabash that has been hollowed out serves as a container both for water and for palm wine in West Africa; pottery jars are used in more arid regions. Nomadic tribes, unable to carry the fragile pottery or cumbersome calabash with them, usually use skin — most often goat or camel — flasks. Among the nomad's domestic items are a wooden headrest to put his head on at night or to be used as a stool; and a staff, which is used to guide the cattle, sheep, or goats, or simply to lean on, as the Somali do. In the south-central part of the Congo, the Binji tribe use a buffalo horn as a

A Somali nomad, with headrest and staff in hand.

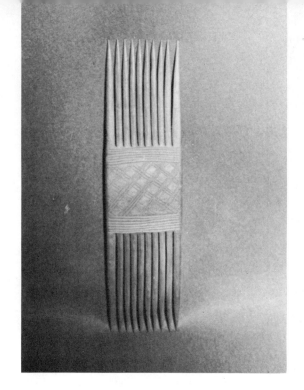

A ten-inch-long wooden comb.

drinking cup for wine. The horn is elaborately carved and decorated with copper wire.

Combs of many different shapes, sizes, and designs, but nearly always made of wood, are found throughout Africa. They usually have about nine to twelve long wooden teeth, sometimes on both ends, or a carved figure, perhaps of an animal or a human head, on one end. A toothbrush is made from an eight-inch stick of wood, sometimes with a carved design on the handle, but flat at the brush end. Fans, so important in hot weather, are seen all over Africa.

This is the house and some of the household items of traditional Africa. However, the modern age is coming to Africa rapidly, and skyscrapers are seen in many cities. The cement, steel, aluminum, and glass of modern industry are needed to build them. The skyscrapers of Africa's main cities look as

Modern architectural forms have been used in building the University of Lagos.

A statue of King Ehengbuda stands under a protective roof outside the palace of the Oba of Benin in Nigeria.

though they belong in Europe or America. The main criticism Africans have of these skyscrapers is that they are not African in design. Some efforts are being made to counter this. The University of Lagos is a good example of the use of curves in modern African architecture. In addition, mosaics and paintings by African artists now decorate the exterior walls of some structures. Often a piece of African sculpture can be seen standing outside a building. Also, more attention is being given to doors, particularly of government buildings and churches; there are good examples of carved wooden doors by African artists.

Perhaps the outcome will be a happy combination of the best the West can offer and the best in African culture.

A modern carved wooden door panel showing a chief and two attendants.

# CHAPTER FIVE

# Religion and Ceremony

Until the relatively modern influence of non-African religions, such as Islam and Christianity, Africans had their own religious beliefs. They still do. African religions are very often described as pagan. While accurate in the sense that, strictly interpreted, "pagan" means "non-Christian; a worshiper of idols," this is not a fair description of the religious beliefs of the African.

They did have idols. But the idols were usually worshiped only as representations of some greater power or force. This invisible power dominated their lives, and they communicated with it through the idols. While they did not worship the idols themselves, it was through the carved idols that the people could act out, express, and communicate their needs, hopes, and prayers to an almighty power. Africans, as people in other continents and of other religions have done, took great care in making these images. This might be compared to the way Christians have made artistic creations of the cross for their altars.

The study of the art created for religious purposes helps us to understand the lives and history of the Africans. It tells us much of how they lived, what they feared, and what was important to them. Tribal life, for example, has always been one of the basic elements in understanding Africa. Tribal customs were closely associated with religious ceremonies, including the creation and use of masks, music, dances, chants, and magical words, or prayers, and special costumes. Various objects were made for use in celebrating birth, in a naming ceremony for a newly born child, at a coming-of-age or a circumcision ceremony, at a marriage or motherhood celebration, on special feast days, and upon a death, or for the singing of "medicine songs." Carved wooden, supposedly magical, staffs with human figures were used by the Senefu in the upper part of the Ivory Coast during fertility rites. Seed-covered headdresses were worn during secret-society rituals by the Angas tribe of northern Nigeria.

A wooden fertility doll from the Ivory Coast, used in religious rites by young brides.

Shrines built to remember the dead, and frequently covered with art objects, are found in parts of West Africa. In some other parts of Africa a dying man is taken into the open country and left to die. Eventually he will be eaten by vultures and hyenas. Thus, he will be spiritually freed, and physically his presence after death will not create a health problem. In the eastern part of Nigeria carved wooden memorials are mounted on stone bases and placed on graves. In Angola soapstone figures, some with leopards' teeth and claws, have long been in use in the same way.

It is important to understand the differences between the various forms of tribalism in Africa. The ceremonies and customs vary considerably from one tribe to another. One aspect of tribal identification that can be interpreted as artistic, in addition to dress and dwellings, is the manner in which some Africans decorate their faces or bodies to identify themselves as belonging to a particular tribe. Elaborate tattoos on the face or stomach, done with ash, sometimes mixed with antimony, are quite extraordinary. In parts of West Africa, the people mark their faces and their bodies. By looking at a man or a woman you can (if you know how to) quickly tell exactly where he or she comes from.

It has also been mentioned that musical instruments — ankle bells or coils of wire, and wooden or metal rods held and struck together to keep the beat of the music — play a part in ceremonies. Then there are the many different types of drums. Some drums, made entirely of wood with a thin slit on top, emit a low tone that carries a great distance. This is one type of drum used for communication. It is sometimes referred to as a "talking

Elaborate markings on the face and arm identify this woman by tribe.

This slit wooden drum is used for communication.

drum." Other drums are covered with hide and leather draw-strings to produce different tones. The Yoruba *gangan* is such an instrument. The more elaborate ones are decorated with Asooke fabric and brass bells.

Other musical instruments include the so-called Hausa piano, which is made of a number of lengths of bamboo in

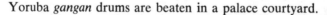

Yoruba *gangan* drums are beaten in a palace courtyard.

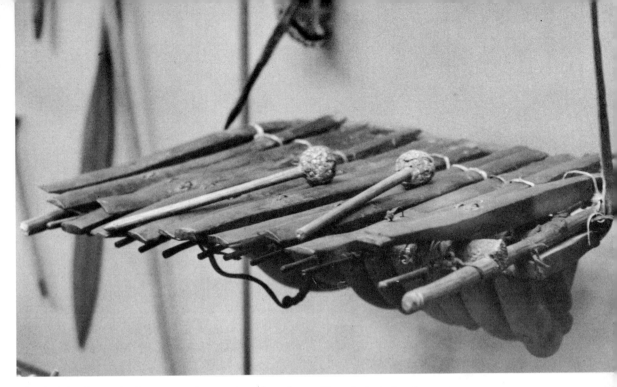

The *balafon* is a xylophone-type instrument that gives off reedy but pleasing notes.

which seeds have been placed, with reed strings tied to the bamboo. The reed strings are plucked with the fingers (usually only the thumbs) and rattled, giving off two different—rattle and string—musical notes. There is the *balafon*, which is the French name for a xylophone-type instrument. Pieces of wood of different lengths are tied onto a wooden frame, and hanging below the frame are gourds that give resonance to the tones struck on the wood with sticks. The Ghana tribe along the western shore of Lake Victoria in Uganda use a log xylophone, different in appearance but played in the same manner.

There are also wooden rattles, metal *gong-gongs, ishaka* (round containers made of cane and containing seeds), thumb (or hand) "pianos," which are blocks of wood, sometimes hollowed out, as in Uganda, with six to eight metal strips which

The bamboo Hausa piano, somewhat more than a foot long, is played both by plucking the reeds strung along its length and by shaking it to make the seeds in the bamboo rattle.

are plucked much in the same manner as the bamboo Hausa "piano." There is another similar instrument called a *molo* by the Yorubas and a *ubo* by the Ibos that is a calabash cut in half onto which a wooden top has been fitted and strips of metal placed much the same as with the thumb "pianos." Horns made of bone or wood are sometimes used by the Chagga tribe of Tanzania. In Muslim areas an eight-foot-long decorated tin horn (called a *kakari*) can be found; in Kano today a representative of the emir appears on his camel as each plane lands and blows his horn to send evil spirits away.

Musical instruments, which will be discussed further in Chapter Nine, play a large part in religious and ceremonial activities of the African. They, of course, provide the background for dances, which are very much part of man's means of expressing his needs and beliefs as well as an unwritten record of history passed down through the years.

# CHAPTER SIX

# Economy

In our lives today, money is not usually thought of as a form of art. However, when we see some of the forms of money used in Africa until quite recent times we can consider them as works of art. Money, by definition, is a standard of value in terms of which commodities are exchanged. (*Moneta* was the name the Romans gave to their silver, coined in the temple of Juno Moneta, 269 B.C.) Money can be a commodity itself, such as gold, silver, or other metals that are made into coins or other objects of value. Cattle, for example, are a sign of wealth in parts of Africa; a "bride price," which a man may have to pay when he marries, is often fixed in terms of a specific number of cattle or of goats, sheep, and so on.

Africans did not use coins until they were colonized by the Europeans. As a medium of exchange they used commodities, objects, that were of value to them. Often the medium of exchange took on a value greater than its actual worth, just as the coins used in the United States today are valued at a price higher than the worth of the metal they contain. For money, Africans used metal shaped into different forms, beads, raffia mats and cloth, shells, weapons and tools, and even rubber balls.

Beads were used in the Congo early in the twentieth century. For example, in 1910 the Shi people of eastern Congo paid five hundred bunches (of ten strings each) of red beads for a cow, while a small pot of beer cost one string. Blue beads had six times the value of the red beads.

Cloth used as a form of money in Africa was called, quite appropriately, "barter cloth." The Mano tribe of Liberia in 1930 paid one bolt of barter cloth for one goat. Also, the women of the Kasai tribe of the Congo embroider designs on raffia cloth which men have woven from raffia-palm fibers. This cloth, sometimes called "Kasai velvet" and worn on ceremonial occasions, was formerly used as money. In Angola the forms of money paid by the Portuguese to Africans during the slave-trading days (nineteenth century) were patterned raffia cloths and cowrie shells.

Rubber balls, usually stuck together, were used as money in the Congo; raffia mats were also used in the Congo, particularly to pay for tribal initiation fees. In the eastern Congo, land snails strung on a raffia string were a form of money.

Iron money, in the shape of useful objects such as spearheads, axes, knives, hoes, and spades, was used in several parts of western Africa. Spear-blade money was, for example, used by the Genya tribe of the eastern Congo. Even nails were sometimes used as money.

The gold weights of Ghana were figures — of people, animals, or other objects — made by the lost-wax process (described in Chapter One). These weights, actually made of brass or bronze, were used by ancient rulers and merchants to weigh gold dust.

Manillas, circular or semicircular sections of metal, were another form of money used in Africa. Some authorities consider them a British innovation; however, it is more likely that the Portuguese introduced the *manilla* to West Africa as a medium of exchange that was in common use for four hundred years. From about 1903 until as late as 1940, the *manilla* was being used as money in remote areas between the Cross and Niger rivers. There are many different sizes, weights, and shapes of *manillas*. The smallest one is about half the size of a dough-

*Manillas* were used as money in West Africa until as recently as 1940.

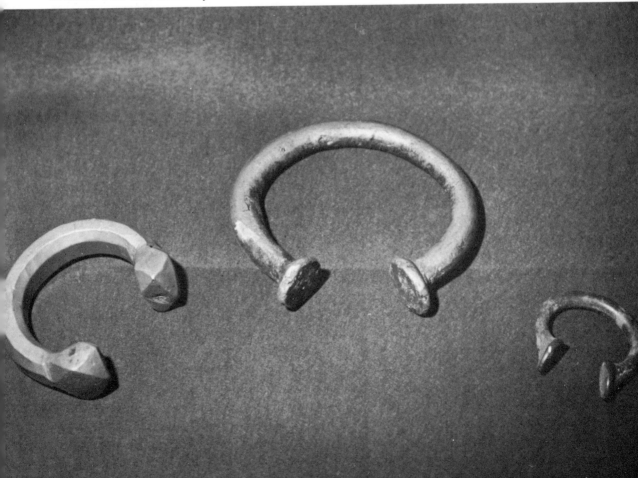

nut, but about a half-inch "bite" is taken out of it. The largest are the King and Queen *manillas,* which are nearly a foot across. *Manillas* were made of bronze, iron, or an alloy, but some are of pure tin. They are often elaborately decorated with designs and were often used for religious and ceremonial purposes.

# CHAPTER SEVEN

# Transportation

Some consideration must be given to the aspects of art in transportation. There is artistry in the basic structure of river, lake, and ocean boats — in their design, shape, and method of construction. Canoes, dugouts, dhows, and outriggers are found in various parts of Africa. The canoe or dugout, not dissimilar to that of the early American Indian, is the major water vehicle in Africa. It is used in river, lake, and even ocean transportation.

The canoes of Lake Chad, made of interwoven sticks and reeds, differ markedly from the dugouts, or river canoes, of the Yorubas and from the canoes that are seen on the Niger River. Outriggers used in parts of East Africa are believed to have been introduced from Indonesia; these were the first vessels used to make the voyage between East Africa and China (Canton) in the first century A.D. The dhow is an Arab vessel used along the Indian Ocean shores of East Africa. East Africans use it for travel between their countries and the Arab lands and India. In villages and even along the west coast cities of Africa the lack of good harbors makes large canoes the only means by which goods and people can be brought ashore from seagoing

Canoe houseboats at the base of the marketplace in Onitsha, along the shores of the Niger River.

vessels. Ceremonial canoe paddles were made by the Itsekiri tribe of Nigeria, who placed them in their shrines as power symbols.

Camels are called the ships of the desert. Many camel saddles are beautiful examples of artwork. Leather harnesses such as those made in Upper Volta often are quite intricately decorated with beads and metalwork. Camel whips are usually made of intertwined strips of dyed leather about four feet long with a woven handle as a grip. The Buduma people who live on an island in Lake Chad kill hippopotamuses with spears and from the hide make camel whips which they sell in Bornu, Nigeria.

Forms of artistic expression are found on lorries (trucks) in West Africa today. Slogans, religious sayings, or warnings painted in bold and fancy letters above the windshield and sometimes on the sides and back of the vehicle are an amusing form of "poster" art. It is with regret that no claims to art can be found in or on automobiles, bicycles, and motorcycles that jam the highways into most large African cities.

# CHAPTER EIGHT

# War and the Hunt

In Africa bows and arrows, spears, shields, clubs, and knives were and are still used as weapons for fighting animals and men; as symbols of authority in ceremonies; as a medium of exchange (money); and for hunting and fishing. The shapes, designs, and composition of these weapons are what make them art. The design of each weapon is peculiar to the tribe that makes and uses it. The Hausa "watchnight" (night watchman) who guards a factory or office building in downtown Lagos, capital of Nigeria, may well be armed with a bow and poison-tipped arrows. His accuracy is undisputed. The Pygmies of the Ituri forest in the Congo are marksmen in their hunt for food in the forest, the arrow always hitting its mark. The Pygmy's bows are decorated with fur from a diadem monkey; the bow-string is rattan. The container used to carry the arrows is made either of wood or more often leather, and it, like the bow, is also decorated with the fur of the diadem monkey. Many tribes in East Africa, from the Sudan to Malawi, use bows and arrows in hunting. And a number of tribes use them to pierce the vein in the neck of their cattle (as do the Masai and Somali) to get blood, which when mixed with milk is an important part of their diet. (The wound is closed with a pack of mud and dung and heals quickly with no harm to the animal.)

Spears are also used for wars and the hunt, although the Masai use them as walking staffs.

A copper knife is carried by the chief of the Mangbetu tribe of the northeastern Congo as a sign of authority. A sword used by the kings of western Africa, such as the Oni of Ife, the Alake of Abeokuta, or the Oba of Benin — in Nigeria — was made purely for religious and ceremonial purposes to symbolize the authority of the ruler over his people. It had no cutting edge and was usually made of cast bronze, very heavy and highly decorated with different geometric designs on the flat surface of the blade and on the handle. In Ghana, objects

Ethiopian shield, knives, and scythelike sword.

Spears, shields, and wooden bludgeons used by warring tribes in parts of central and northern Africa.

such as a man or an animal carved on the scabbard of the chief's state sword tell a story. However, some swords were made for warfare as well as ceremonial purposes, as were those of the Chagga (in Tanzania), carried in thick leather scabbards and belts decorated with beadwork and metal chains.

The shield belongs to nomadic tribes, but most often is identified with certain tribes in East Africa such as the Masai. Border clashes between tribes or within a country over the use of a water hole are going on today; shield and weapon are used to defend one's "rights" or to survive. However, they are also used in ceremonial activities, particularly dances, as done by the Watusi of Burundi.

Knives serve many purposes. Some are weapons. Others, with a small cutting blade, are used for carving. Various types are used to skin animals and prepare food. Machetes may be weapons or tools. Machetes are needed for such things as cropping the fields for cassava roots and slicing the cactuslike blades of sisal from their stalks. Knives and machetes are sometimes all metal, pounded into shape over a fire and sharpened on a stone; then the handle and sometimes the blade is etched with a design. Frequently the handle is made of wood or bone.

As proof that knives, among other weapons, are considered art today, one gallery in New York sold in 1969 three Bakuba knives from the Congo, one "with tapering blade, and knopped wooden handle bound with copper"; another, "an Azande knife with eccentric curving blade"; and the third "a Ubangi knife with long, curving blade." The three sold as a set for $250, while at an auction at the same gallery two years before, three similar knives from Gabon were sold for $140. The appreciation, in price, of art is going up with increased demand.

With firearms, a comparatively recent invention of man, came cow-horn gunpowder containers — frequently decorated with strands of beads — that are now considered attractive collectors' items.

Armor in Africa? Yes. There are still ceremonial occasions for which the ancient armor introduced to Timbuktu by the Crusaders is worn.

# CHAPTER NINE

# Entertainment

Today people in the West have a great deal of leisure time to spend as they want, to entertain or be entertained. They can dance, listen to music, go to the movies, the opera, the theater, the ballet, or concerts. They have the whole field of active sports as entertainment. Then there are home games: cards, backgammon, chess, checkers, dominoes. And, of course, there is television. Not all entertainment is art, although this point is debatable, according to the individual's taste.

A man struggling in and with his environment, living at a subsistence level, has little time for play; but, even so, he cannot work all the time. He needs to relax. This has been true throughout history. A game of chance and skill, played on "boards" (some plain and some elaborately carved in wood with added metal decorations) that is played by Africans is called *mancala*. Actually, this is the Arabic name of the board-with-holes-played-with-seeds game that is known by many different names. Played in the Middle East in pre-Mohammedan times, it is now played throughout Africa. It is called Ayo in Yoruba (Nigeria and Dahomey), Wari by the Liberians, Omweso in Uganda, and Bao by the Laisami tribe of Kenya.

Dances and music were generally associated with religious or ceremonial occasions, although occasionally they were performed for pleasure. In either case the composition of the music, the staging of the dances, and the costumes and other ornamental apparatus that were worn in connection with a particular celebration were illustrative of the art of the particular society. Some "theatrical" entertainment also took place in the form of acted-out stories of wars, or an episode in history such as a famine or flood, or the reign of a powerful ruler. Naming ceremonies (of children), baptisms, circumcision ceremonies when a boy or girl came of age, births, marriages, and fu-

A man playing *ayo* counts the seeds he has won.

nerals were all occasions for entertainment, with the pomp and circumstance that each deserved.

Today many Africans perform modern dances while at home or at a party. The modern dance of West Africa is called High Life. At a social gathering, people rise to move about to the beat of the drum and horn, each dancer shuffling his feet and pumping his arms without touching his partner. Does it sound familiar?

Musical instruments have already been discussed in the chapter on religion and ceremony. However, let us consider them further under the category of entertainment. Let us take one country in Africa — Ethiopia — and examine its musical instruments. (Ethiopia became independent about A.D. 1040, or before William the Conqueror [1027–87] invaded England in 1066.) Only percussion instruments are used for religious music; nonreligious music is played with string, wind, and percussion instruments. Usually a moral or instructive poem is recited in accompaniment with religious music. Instruments found in Ethiopia include the *begenna, kerar, masank'o, washint, embilta, malaket,* and *kabaro*. The first three are string instruments. The *begenna*, which looks like a harp, has only one string. Wind instruments include the *washint, embilta,* and *malaket*; the latter is a sort of trumpet and is used in religious processions or to call flocks together. The *kabaro* is a drum made of skin on an irregularly shaped frame.

This gives an idea of the kind and variety of musical instruments that can be found in one African country. However, there are many variations of these instruments as well as many different kinds in other parts of Africa.

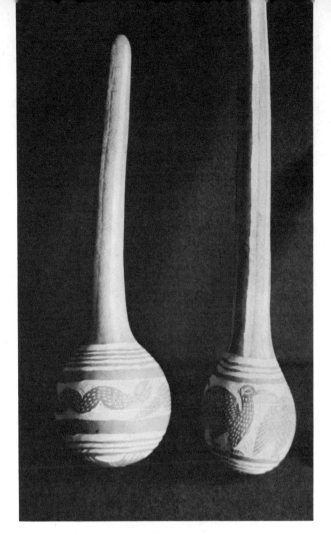

Calabash rattles with decorative designs contain seeds that produce a soft musical sound.

Drums are found everywhere and are included in most musical groups as the basis for the rhythm. Drums are made from a variety of materials, not only wood and skin. In Liberia there is a drum made from tortoise shell. The Zulus used their hide shields as drums. The *sakara* in Nigeria is called a drum although it more closely resembles a tambourine: a circle of fired clay is covered with a goatskin, attached with wooden pegs, string, or grass. Frequently the tops of these *sakaras* are painted with scenes of the tropical rain forest or village life. The *dundun* or *gangan* drum of Nigeria is particularly decora-

Wooden carvings of a flutist and two drummers. The center figure is beating a *gangan* drum.

tive and tonal, and is used for ceremonial purposes as well as to send messages. Drums in Uganda are covered with zebra skin, cowhide, python, buck, or lizard skin. They range from 4 to 42 inches high and from 5 to 36 inches in diameter.

There are other horns besides that of the Hausa, previously mentioned. The Marakwet tribe of Kenya use a carved kudu antelope horn to call the people together to dig irrigation ditches. The Acholi tribe in Uganda have a four-foot trumpet made of wood, covered with cowhide, and blown from the side rather than the end. The Buganda tribe has a black buck horn, also side blown, that is about two feet long. In the Congo an ivory whistle is used to send messages.

# CHAPTER TEN

# Contemporary Art

Contemporary art must be considered in two categories: (1) commercial art and (2) art for art's sake. Commercial art must be thought of as functional; it is produced to make money. Most of this type of art is what has been called "airport art," mass-produced and generally poor in quality, for sale to tourists visiting Africa and for export to be sold in shops throughout the United States and Europe. Art produced for art's sake alone is just beginning in Africa. Art made by the artist for his own pleasure has only become possible by a growth of the local African economies, art education in African universities, grants from foreign foundations and individuals, and the introduction abroad of African art into international galleries. It must be kept in mind that much of the art for art's sake in Africa today is created with the purpose of enhancing the culture in the country of origin.

Most of the commercial art of today comes from East Africa (Kenya, Tanzania, and Uganda) and from Nigeria, Guinea, Ghana, and the Ivory Coast. Commercial art from Africa falls into the following types of arts and crafts: stone-work, pottery, textiles; grass, straw, sisal, and bark work; wood-

This modern free-standing forty-six-inch-high figure was carved by the Makonde tribe of East Africa.

en carvings of thornwood, ebony, pine, walnut, among others; paintings, metal sculpture, glasswork, brass lost-wax figures, hides and skins, meerschaum, ivory carvings, and other items made from animal bone, hair, teeth, claws, and horns.

The amount of African stonework sculpture, both old and new, is limited and found mainly in Nigeria, the Congo, Sierra Leone, and Rhodesia. Some is also found in Kenya. Stonework is produced in the form of animals, figures, and beads. Today soapstone figures are found in as geographically separated areas as Gabon and Rhodesia. In Kisii, Kenya, attractive white stone carvings are made in limited but exportable quantities. Rhodesian stone carvings range from six inches to two feet high and are made of heavy greenish, brown, gray, or purple stone. Before the coming of the white man to Africa, stonecutting took place in many parts of the continent, including Sierra Leone, the Kisii area of Guinea, around Ife in western Nigeria, on the Upper Cross River near the Cameroon border of eastern Nigeria, and on the south bank of the Congo.

Pottery is found throughout Africa. Best noted for pottery are the Meta and Babesi tribes in Cameroon; the Oubanguian potters in the Central African Republic; the female potters near Brazzaville, the Congo, who model clay with their hands (as do the potters in Abomey, Dahomey) rather than on a wheel; and the pottery-training center at Abuja in Nigeria. Pottery has been an art of many ancient civilizations. The manufacture of earthenware existed among the Hebrews as an honorable occupation. The power of the potter over the clay as a symbol of the power of God over the world is described by Jeremiah, 605 B.C. Earthenware was made by the ancient Egyptians, Assyri-

Pottery, an art of many ancient civilizations, is still popular in Africa. This pottery market is in Mogadishu, capital of Somali.

ans, Greeks, Etruscans, and Romans. In the United States the art of pottery in the Southwest is about 1,600 years old and served the same uses as does the pottery of the Africans: as storage jars, cooking pots, and ceremonial vessels. It is still not at all uncommon in Africa to see a woman returning from a well or reservoir with a pottery jar filled with water balanced on her head.

Handwoven textiles and their functional use in clothing have already been described in considerable detail in Chapter

Two. As a commercial exportable item, African handwoven or embroidered cloths are being made into Western- or American-styled clothing, and into accessories such as handbags, men's ties, eyeglass cases, cushions, and even bookmarks. The difficulty in bringing African handwoven products to a large American market is the cost and limited production capability; varying quality, size, and colors of each piece; and the inability of most handwoven materials to lend themselves to machine cutting for mass production, even if the material could be produced. This means additional cost for production by hand of items made from the fabrics.

Fibrous materials are used to make roofing, fences, and mat shields for local use, and baskets, table place mats, hats, coasters, bags, belts, shoes, and even cushions for sale both in Africa and abroad. The most common materials are banana palm, raffia, papyrus, sisal, and sorghum. Some baskets, such as those woven from sisal by the Tusi women in Uganda, are so tightly woven that they can even be used as containers for milk.

Africa is best known for its wood carvings. An important factor must be considered when discussing wood carvings. They are not durable. That is why there are very few really old wood carvings. They may be about three hundred years old or so at the very most, but they are called old even when they were made only thirty years ago. Carvings decay and are eaten away, particularly when still in use in an African village, by termites that bore their way through the wood. Another damaging factor is the climate — either too dry or too wet. What must also be considered is that when exported, usually 25 percent of the wooden carvings crack badly. They just cannot withstand

A modern eighteen-inch-high ebony carving of the head of an *oba* resembles many ancient Benin bronzes.

the changes of temperature and humidity; or, in the case of new carvings, the wood is still "green." Nevertheless, the majority of the art exported from Africa in recent years has been made of wood, masks and animal figures in particular. They are made from different woods; the type of wood, as well as the workmanship, determines the price. Ebony carvings come from West Africa, and are usually priced higher than the pine of the eastern part of the continent because of the cost of the wood as well as the cost of labor. For example, a miniature carved wooden animal that costs ten cents in Nairobi, Kenya, costs thirty cents in Lagos, Nigeria. Carved wood items nave a diverse functional purpose. They take such forms as trays, bowls, shoehorns, tables, lamps, cigarette boxes, bookends, and key chains; but they still are the most ornamental insofar as a foreigner is concerned. There is only a limited African market for arts and crafts made to be sold as commercial items.

In considering wood carvings in Africa as a commercial art, let us take one example: the thornwood carvings of Nigeria. Let us see how the art of thornwood carving began and developed into a business. One of the originators of thornwood carving is Justice D. Akeredolu, born in 1915 in Owe. He is now working in the Department of Antiquities in the museum in Lagos. Joseph A. Lamuren, in Shagamu, now has thirty-seven carvers on his staff, making thornwood carvings for domestic sale in Nigeria as well as for export around the world. Lamuren, son of an Asooke weaver and carver of *iroku* wood, started carving figures out of thornwood when in school. At first Lamuren would use his slate to polish the surface of a piece of thornwood he had picked off a bush. He would write the names of his schoolmates on the polished wood and frequently decorate the article with a carved figure. Then, one day a British government inspector saw Lamuren's work and asked him to make a dozen figures for him for which he paid him a pound ($2.80 at that time). This started Lamuren's career of carving. He formed a partnership with Justice Akeredolu in the early 1930's, but is now on his own. At first he used a rough leaf to smooth off the surfaces, but eventually modernized his methods to include glue and sandpaper. Each of the figures he makes today represents some aspect of village life: drummers, dancers, a woman carrying a pot or sticks, a Muslim reading the Koran, a woman dyeing raffia, a woman weaving on an Akwete

Joseph Lamuren's workers carve intricate thornwood pieces.

loom, a trader carrying his wares on his head, a woman cooking soup, two women pounding yams, a boy hoeing, a farmer feeding chickens, and large multiple-figure carvings of canoes with people, dancers in a circle, an entire village scene, and chess sets with each figure resembling a Yoruba tribesman.

Another material that has served many purposes and has been carved in different ways is the calabash. It was used originally — and still is — as a container for liquid. However, cala-

A bowl made from a calabash.

Decorative calabash pieces cut into the shapes of a bird and a tortoise.

bashes are also cut and shaped into bowls, animal figures, spoons, and rattles, all decorated with geometric designs and sometimes animals and birds. Thus the calabash becomes a part of the home, religious, and ceremonial life of the African, is used in entertainment, and is a popular tourist item. Designs made on calabashes are done by burning the shell with a hot metal rod. Sometimes cowrie shells or leather and fabric are placed around the handle (root) of the calabash. Large calabashes are made into musical instruments called *agbe* (Nigerian) or *lilolo* (Congo). Calabash seeds inside a dried gourd produce a rattling sound when shaken.

Paintings in Africa include oils, watercolors, sketches, and brush paintings. In the coastal areas of West Africa, from Senegal to the Congo and across Africa to Nairobi, Kenya, brush paintings, which are said to have originated in the Congo and to have been painted with a flamingo feather, are sold. Not only are they now exported by traders from the Congo but the style has been adopted by others. They are nearly always painted on rectangular sheets of thick rough paper, usually black, but also yellow, green, blue, and red. Common subjects are men hunting, birds, and village scenes. Sometimes the brush paintings are on black cloth, stretched onto a wooden frame. Sketched or painted postal and greeting cards done by Africans are being sold today.

The brass lost-wax process has been described. Today, lost-wax figures are made in Ghana, Dahomey, and the Ivory Coast, as well as in other parts of West Africa (Nigeria and Cameroon). The brass figures from these countries tend to find their way into the export market more than those from other areas.

The Bida beads have also been described. They are in considerable demand outside of Africa today, even though they are much more expensive than beads made of other materials, such as seeds and plastic, from the Caribbean and the Far East.

Meerschaum is a mineral that looks like white clay. Chemically it is a hydrous magnesium silicate that is used to make pipes. There are only two places in the world where it is mined: in Turkey and along the Tanzania-Kenya border. The mines in Turkey are on the surface, while in Africa they are underground. The best pipes are made of solid meerschaum; a cheaper pipe is made of pressed meerschaum chips. Some pipes are made entirely of meerschaum. Others have only a meerschaum bowl; the rest of the pipe is of wood or of wood and calabash. Pipes with a Sherlock Holmes-style curve are especially popular.

Calabash also is used to make bowls for East African meerschaum pipes.

Hides and skins are made into clothing (including coats), shoes, and other wearing apparel such as belts, watch straps, sandals, and headbands. Other items are either finished natural skin (such as elephant, snake, lizard, ostrich, and crocodile) or fur (leopard, lion, cheetah, gazelle, and panther). There are note pads, pen sets, change purses, tobacco pouches, coasters, luggage, cigarette boxes, golf-club covers, wallets, billfolds, handbags, key rings, cushions, saddle seats, drum tables, briefcases, and wastepaper baskets. The majority of these products come from East Africa, particularly from Kenya, through Chad (where the panther is found). Morocco leather is so called because it was first traded in Morocco. However, the leather did not originate in Morocco, but came from Sokoto in northern Nigeria. The Morocco leather was that of the red goat of Sokoto.

Other items made from animals include ivory (elephant-tusk) figures, boxes, and jewelry. Some animals' teeth, such as those of the leopard or lion, are used to make charms, pins, and cuff links, while a hippo tooth is made into a bottle opener. Claws of the lion or leopard also are used as jewelry items. The horn of a cow is made into a lamp in the shape of a bird; the horns of the one-foot-high dik-dik gazelle are used to make brooches, cuff links, and letter openers. The hairs from the end of the tail of an elephant or giraffe are tightly wound together to make bracelets or are fitted into gold and made into rings. Even animals' bones are used for tourist art; warthog or cow bones are made into canes.

As a material for commercial art, copper must not be forgotten. In the Congo copper pendants and bracelets with lion,

Hides and skins are dried and made into a number of useful and interesting items. This leatherworker is starting work on a handbag.

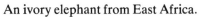

An ivory elephant from East Africa.

elephant, or hippo designs are made, as are copper wall plaques with attractive natural or op-art designs. In addition, they are often traded across the border and sold to exporters in Zambia. Some people believe that wearing copper helps arthritis; some just like the look of copper. Copper has also been used by the Congolese to make frying pans with a cow horn as a handle.

It is interesting to note how many of the commercial items made for international sale are functional even though they are commercial and may be modern in concept. Many of these objects carry on the old traditions, while still very often — as in the case of the lost-wax process — maintaining their original beauty or naturalness.

In conclusion, we must consider "art for art's sake" in Africa. It will be remembered that at the beginning of this book, and throughout, the point has been made that Africans did not make objects that we consider art for art's sake but for a purpose, with a function in their society, their lives, and their time. However, there is now emerging, in parts of Africa, art for art's sake in some forms, namely, sculpture, architecture, mosaics, and painting. The number of African artists has risen sharply in the past decade. Out-of-doors murals are frequently found, sometimes in the most unexpected places. However, painting and mosaics (now manufactured in Africa) are used both as abstracts and as illustrative murals and are most frequently found in central squares of cities or on government or office buildings.

Some very fine modern African painters and sculptors are known not only in their own country but in Europe and America. The Congolese Augustine Bakome had thirteen paintings

Africans are proud of the work of their modern sculptors.

on display at the Pepsi-Cola exhibit in New York in 1961. At the same exhibit, two other Congolese, D. Bomolo and Nzita, each had several paintings on display. Ethiopian Afewerk Tekle designed the window for the Military Academy at Harar, Ethiopia. He also did the sculptures in the New Imperial Palace of the emperor, and mural paintings for the Cathedral of St. George and St. Trinity. The Nigerian Ben Enwonwu, an Ibo, has not only done a number of important pieces of sculpture that decorate buildings in Nigeria, such as the statue of "Shongo," God of Thunder, in front of the ECN (Electricity Corporation of Nigeria) Building in Lagos, but also worked, in 1961, on several large sculptures for the Mirror Building in London. Felix Idubor, a Bini from Nigeria, carved the doors for the ten-story cooperative building in Ibadan, Nigeria, and for the new National Hall in Lagos. Akinola Lesekan is one of the earlier modern Nigerian artists, born in 1916. In 1945 he had an exhibition in London of paintings on African life; he also painted a portrait of Sir Winston Churchill which he sold for $700. Israel Ala, who studied under Ben Enwonwu, and in London at Bromley Art College, has sold a number of his works abroad. The Tanzanian Elimo P. Najau is famous for his murals. A painting by Sam J. Ntiro, also from Tanzania, is in the Museum of Modern Art, New York. Alexander Atori of Uganda did three large mural panels in Uganda House, in London, that depicted "Karamajong Dancers," "Cattle Grazing," and "Cotton Farming."

The modern art of Africa created for aesthetic rather than purely functional purposes has been strongly influenced by European style although the subject matter and interpretation is definitely African.

Although international recognition and the dimension of pure pleasure in art have now come to Africa, the old tradition of functional art remains. Art in Africa thereby holds an enviable position — it plays a vital part in the lives of all the people.

# Bibliography

## BOOKS

Davidson, Basil. *The Lost Cities of Africa*. Boston: Little, Brown and Company, 1959.

Dietz and Olatunji. *Musical Instruments of Africa*. New York: The John Day Company, Inc., 1965.

Elsevier. *Atlas du Congo Belge et du Ruanda-Urundi*. Paris: 1955.

Fage, J.D. *An Atlas of African History*. London: Edward Arnold, Ltd., 1958.

Fagg, William. *Nigerian Images*. New York: Frederick A. Praeger, Inc., 1963.

Fagg, William and Plass, Margaret. *African Sculpture*. New York: E.P. Dutton & Co., Inc., 1964.

Holas, B. *Arts de la Cote d'Ivoire*. Paris: Presses Universitaires de France, 1966.

Horrabin, J.F. *An Atlas of Africa*. New York: Frederick A. Praeger, Inc., 1960.

Marcus, Rebecca B. *Prehistoric Cave Paintings*. New York: Franklin Watts, Inc., 1968.

Parrinder, Geoffrey. *African Mythology*. London: Paul Hamlyn, Ltd., 1967.

Segy, Ladislas. *African Sculpture*. New York: Dover Publications, Inc., 1958.

Simmons, Frederick J. *Northwest Ethiopia*. Madison, Wisconsin: University of Wisconsin Press, 1960.

Thomas, Elizabeth Marshall. *The Harmless People*. New York: Alfred A. Knopf, Inc., 1959.

Ullendorff, Edward. *The Ethiopians*. London: Oxford University Press, 1960.

Wassing, Rene S. *African Art*. New York: Harry N. Abrams, Inc., 1968.

World Crafts Council. *World Crafts — A Mid-Twentieth-Century Survey*. 1966.

ARTICLES AND OTHER SOURCES

Bahti, Tom. "Southwest Indian Arts and Crafts," Flagstaff, Arizona: KC Publications, 1966.

Beier, Ulli. "Art in Nigeria," Cambridge University Press, 1960.

————. "Sacred Wood Carvings from One Small Yoruba Town." Lagos, Nigeria: *Nigeria Magazine,* 1957.

Brown, Evelyn S. "Africa's Contemporary Art and Artists," New York: Harom Foundation, 1966.

Buffalo Books, Ltd. "The Sculpture of Western Africa," London.

Connah, Graham. "Classic Excavation in Northeast Nigeria," *Illustrated London News*, Oct. 14, 1967.

————. "Polished Stone Axes in Benin," Apapa, Nigeria: Nigeria National Press, 1964.

Ethiopian Airlines, brochure published by. "Musical Instruments — Ethiopia," 1967.

Gainsborough Galleries. "Art in Africa," Johannesburg, South Africa, 1960.

Horton, Robin. "The Gods as Guests," Lagos, Nigeria: *Nigeria Magazine*, March, 1960.

Ministry of Culture and Community Development. "Uganda Crafts," Kampala, Uganda, 1965.

Ministry of Trade and Industry. "Industrial Potentialities of Northern Nigeria," Kaduna, Nigeria, 1963.

National Geographic. "Preserving the Treasures of Olduvai Gorge," and "Proud Primitives, the Nuba People," Washington, D.C., Vol. 130, No. 5, November, 1966.

Nigerian Museum. "The Art of Ife," Lagos, Nigeria, 1955.

————. "Nigerian Antiquities," Lagos, Nigeria, 1959.

Sweeney, James J. "The Beauties and Uses of African Art," *New York Times Book Review*, January 12, 1969.

# Index

94